CROSSING STREAMS ON ROCKS

CROSSING STREAMS ON ROCKS

Poems by David Davis

Bard Brook Press   ◆   Belchertown, Massachusetts

Crossing Streams on Rocks
Copyright © 2011 by David Davis

Published by Bard Brook Press
Belchertown, Massachusetts 01007
www.bardbrookpress.com

First Edition
April 2011

Book design by Eileen Klockars

ISBN-13: 978-0-9834931-0-5

Printed in the United States of America

Dedication

To Hal and Kirby, who filled our house with songs and rhymes

Acknowledgements

A great many of the poems in this book have been improved by the suggestions made by the amazing members of the Powow River Poets poetry workshop, founded by Rhina Espaillat.

Alex Bruskin, Wendy Davis, Rebecca Ferare, Luxman Krishnamoorthy, Alfred Nicol, my parents, and Wendy Williams provided insightful comments on prior drafts of this book.

Eileen and Bruce Klockars produced the book and improved its form and content immeasurably.

"A.I." and "An Eternal Golden Braid" were originally published in *The Flea*.

"From The Belvedere Tower" was originally published in *Mastodon Dentist*.

Contents

CROSSING STREAMS ON ROCKS

Canine Theology

In the beginning there was food
and there were no doors
and there were dogs
and dogs smelled dogs
and dogs smelled like dogs
and it was good.

Now there are dogs and there is food
and them, and they give dogs food
but they do not smell dogs
and they do not smell like dogs
but they open the door
and they are sometimes good.

In the time that can't yet be smelled
there will be dogs and there will be food
and maybe them and maybe something else
that gives dogs food
and smells dogs
and smells like dogs
and opens the door
and goes out to a world wild with smells
and lifts its leg and all is good.

Massachusetts January

I hate to see that evening sun go down
on winter nights when we need warmth to glow.
The pallid glimmer of the lights in town
is not enough to fool our eyes. They know
reflections off the sheets of snow and ice
laid down in layers by this week's, last week's storm
are powerless to help us, being twice
removed from sun and times when we were warm.
The worst of winter isn't that it's cold
or that next to it summer seems to shine.
It's that our will congeals and so we old
grow weary of our options, uninclined
to fly to Florida, lean back, and reach
for suntan lotion on a hot white beach.

Young Joy

Joy arrives sooner than nine months
    but can crawl away at any time.
You must expect some contractions—
    joy is blocked if your head is too large.
Joy must be bathed and tended to
    (it helps to squeak rubber ducks in the tub.)
You should feed joy pureed experience
    and make funny noises or she won't eat.
Hold joy gently, pat her on the back,
    and you will like what she spits up.

How the Spring

How the south wind blows again
   How the snowbanks melt
How the cold frame holds the sun
   How the warmth is felt

How the dusk lasts into night
   How the darkness fades
How the grass reflects the light
   How the tufts are made

How the showers fall for days
   How the gutters flow
How the mud is washed away
   How the pebbles glow

How the ladder hugs the tree
   How the branch is broken
How the saw blade sets it free
   How the soul is woken

Seize the Moment

I place a marker in time on now.
It is instantly jerked into the past.
I throw a marker ahead one minute
and step aside as it picks up speed,
hurtling to its eternal home.
I nail a marker to this now.
It explodes, sending shards in all directions.
I place a now in a lead-lined vault
embedded in concrete, then open the door.
There is nothing left but an oily spot
fading fast, and a hint of lavender.

Boston Marathon 2004

Twenty down six more, I walked for a bit
but a teammate said Run so I ran without thought,
hearing voices wrapped in a strange roaring.

How Are You? they asked at the finish Okay
but they led me away to the first aid tent:
forty-five minutes in green-tinted light,

packed in ice, sucking on emerald fluids.
A Kenyan beside me, better time than mine,
lay prone with I.V. tubes stuck in his arm.

I wandered a bit, climbed the stairs late at night.
A Very Warm Day they said on the news.
For the rest of the week I still heard that roaring.

Sonnet with Horse

A quatrain made of one strong rhyme and glue
to hold the lines that long to fly apart;
a weaker rhyme that somehow has to do;
a horse that hates to pull its racing cart.

Another quatrain stronger than the first,
appealing to the senses—something red
flutters from its mane while bubbles burst
inside the spittle hanging from its head.

A volta taking us from there to here
while the horse rebelliously plods;
one good turn deserves another near
a final couplet written by the gods:

these enterprises fit our grand design
if horse and sonnet reach the finish line.

An Eternal Golden Braid

She leans forward slightly,
her yellow hair plaited in braids,
hands typing at the keyboard.

She places her subject in a dark-lit room,
his hair unkempt, his face unshaved,
as slovenly as her ex-husband.

He scratches the paper with his pen,
scattering words on the page
like garden slugs, oozing toward his hand.

She pushes him back into deeper gloom
and flicks away garden slugs
as they appear on her keyboard.

I stop her movement a moment too late.
Garden slugs glide up my pencil
and disappear, leaving one yellow hair behind.

The First Bird

The young bird knows it is the first
to feel hunger. It assumes the cries
of its nestmates are mimicry,
mindless copies of its true pain.

The juvenile knows it is the first
to soar in flight. It sees the others
scooping air, their weak flutters
pale renderings of its own skill.

The adult bird knows it is the first
to build a nest and fill it with eggs,
to see cracks spread from a pecking beak,
the first young bird flop into the world.

Intermediaries

A violet oozes purple tint
    that colors touch

A rock abrades the fingerprints
    so all feels rough

Inhale the jasmine—nothing else—
    the flower smothers

Without consent, some things use us
    To blend with others

Baggage Handlers

They collect your baggage:
your fear of conflict,
the reason you won't talk to your friend again,
the tightness you feel at that corner on State Street.

They lock it all in a storage compartment,
out of touch during the flight.
On landing you can retrieve your baggage
from the carousel as you exit Security.

Very few passengers notice this sign:
All unclaimed baggage will be confiscated,
removed, and ultimately destroyed.

Larkspur

All the cows were facing north but one.
Larkspur was her lodestone. As she ate,
the drug compelled her to stare at the sun,
to kick and howl and fiercely ruminate.
She spent the night hallucinating hay
and milky ways and blazing waves of grain.
She saw the young males deftly led away
and felt the current coursing through each brain.
Why should the cows depend on metal hands
to steal the fluid before their udders ache?
Why should the fences limit where each stands,
and why does this seem normal when awake?
Larkspur drew these uncowlike thoughts forth
but when it faded she knew to face north.

From the Belvedere Tower

I look west at grasslands, the river,
the ancient forest. I can hear
the exuberant calls of siskins and bobolinks.
She looks east at the growing city,
clouded in dust from construction. She can hear
deals being made for further expansion,
the price of everything shouted out as it changes.

Beau Geste

You let the letter blow away
and I, mistaking your intent,
lunged by reflex after it,
nearly ruining the day.

At least the gesture wasn't lost.
When I saw your face I tossed
it up again, higher than you,
as if that's what I'd meant to do.

Homecoming

Returned from Bagdad not sure where I was:
Head overseas, body jetlagged, feet
Covered with desert dust. Went fishing

Derby Creek's foam-covered pools,
like knotholes along the canyon's grain.

Same wet branches, same guardian spruce,
same fallen logway, same numb worm,

same tug on the line. My ghost and I
felt the trout pulling us
out of old undertows, home.

The Radical Indeterminacy of Translation

I don't know what it means,
the woodcock's flight up, twittering,
the spirals overhead as he descends
in twilight. Does she know what it means,
waiting in the grass for his return?

his the loudest, his the highest,
his the widest circles overhead

A coupling in dusk and she flies off.
He'll never see the eggs or young.
I don't think he knows what it means,
stamping in the grass, nasally peenting,
shaking his wings out to ascend again.

Mrs. Simmons

Some people say I talk too much.
As long as you're talking you know you're alive,
like the death of our cat—it just stopped purring.
No one ever died talking
or if they did they were hit by a car
so I keep it up but I make it lively—
I tell how the Smiths both look for it
outside their marriage in the same motel,
which farm stands don't grow their tomatoes,
how the council in its last meeting
voted to let the crooks into town,
which young wife put her man underground,
the things about you you'd not like spread around.

Knight Getting a Quest

I said hello pretty lady, can you tell me what you think?
No air to breathe no trails to walk no water fit to drink.
Your skies are brown your lakes are down your home's under a mall.
Hear the chainsaws coming and your tallest redwoods fall?
Now that we've crossed the moas and the boas off your list
you must be feeling something and I bet extremely pissed,
so tell me what you want and maybe I can lend a hand.
Just give me some direction in words I can understand.

She said nothing.

I said tell me what the answer is and I'll be set to go.
I can help, I've got the power, if you let me know
your plan to turn the tide, to make it live, to help return
to how it was—a perfect place—I simply want to learn
the way to fix the future with sustainability,
or I could clone dimetrodons and I could set them free
to walk the walks and stalk the streets and bring the buildings down
if you would give the word but you don't move or make a sound.

She said nothing.

I said I love your world of wonder and your flowing robes of green.
I want to halt the mass destruction, smash the black machine.
I can drive behind their lines and spike the loggers' trees.
I can pour sand in their tanks, set traps to break their knees.
I can fight a battle to restore your ancient ways.
A commando, I'm your Rambo at the end of days.
I can destroy the very forces that are destroying you.
Just move your hand, speak a command, and tell me what to do.

She said…

Walk into the woods until you find a place that's still.
Sit there without thinking, without any words until
you know the trees and understand the stooping of a hawk.
Do that for several seasons and then come back and let's talk.

Thousands Flee Eruption

I like the way Wallace Stevens
stored up titles in a notebook,
assigning one at random
when he completed a poem.

The Russian Poem

I heard a reading of a Russian poem.
It felt like a box of plates dropped and broken.
Perhaps it was meant to feel that way.
Perhaps Russians model poems on breaking plates,
or this poet was an unusual Russian
for whom breaking plates was a means of protest
or a commentary on social conditions.
When my turn came I dropped a bag of socks.

First Encounter

1. The Aliens View Pyramids from Space

Their onboard scanners analyzed
the large stone shapes. Readouts foretold
itching rock dust, theocracy,
fascination with pointed forms.
The crew melded and changed course
toward islands: soft-shelled crabs,
sand under flippers, humid air,
monuments made from scented woods.

2. The Aliens Are Given a Gift

The kahuna held out a statue.
The aliens melded, collapsed their legs,
thrust olfactory tubes forward.
A hoot of delight circled the meld.
The form, carved by the king's best sculptor,
meant nothing to them, but the blended esters
mixed in the oils made them ecstatic,
the finest art they had ever smelled.

3. The Aliens Visit the Beach

The aliens, in meld and out of it,
rippled their flippers deep in black sand
and waited, rooted for a full day-cycle.
The villagers used them as penalty posts,
riding the waves between them to shore.
The aliens sensed the tidal patterns,
the rise and fall behind the noise,
in shared statistical awareness.

4. The Aliens Depart at Sunset

The aliens went for a final swim,
using scents to repel the sharks.
They popped from the water onto shore
and blended a farewell gift for the village.
Each alien held a coconut fragment
destined for its clan's scent vaults.
Their ship rose above the palms
as the humans writhed in farewell.

The Waterfall

I left my cubicle and those grey things—
the bugs we couldn't fix, the deadlines passed—
to drive four hours and camp near Poncha Springs,
well off a road I always took too fast.

Next day I ate and left at dawn to hike
a trail I chose at random from a map.
Passed once too often by a mountain bike,
I left the path and climbed the ridge. A gap

opened on a way down to a stream.
I followed it, and then I heard a sound.
Aspen-dappled, moving in a dream,
I ducked beneath limbs, made my way around

the powdered trunks and fairy trumpet stalks,
the cinquefoil and columbine and rose,
toward a booming coming from the rocks.
A final wall of briars tore my clothes.

I broke through to a pool beneath a falls,
a hidden place that no one ever knew.
Reverberating thunder filled the walls
of rock that hid the waterfall from view.

I do not know how long I stood in mist
and sound and memory with my mind caught
on something that, somehow, my life had missed
with no awareness of the loss—the thought

that earthbound streams can leap into the air,
turn into rainbows falling like bouquets,
in roaring coruscation land, prepare
for normal life, grow calm, and flow away.

From a Writer Who Sees Colors Poorly

If one of the hunters is color blind,
the group will return carrying more meat.

If one member of a wartime team
scrutinizing photographs can't see colors,
the team will find more camouflaged tanks.

If one in a collection of poems about colors
has no color in it, the collection is improved.
Colors love to distract our eyes
from the truth of an object's form.

Meeting of Two Minds

Two cars at once drove down our road last year.
One was red and one was rusting brown.
They met head-on and stopped and it was clear
that one of them would have to give up ground.
Our lane's not wide enough for two to pass.
Most days we saw no more than one go by.
The man got out. The woman gunned the gas
in neutral, on our road less travelled by.
We could see them point and hear them talk
as they debated aspects of their plight.
At last the woman drove up on our walk
and gestured as the man roared out of sight.
It was exciting. Now more cars turn round
since I took the NARROW ROAD signs down.

Black Swifts

A long meeting in North Carolina.
Very long. My brain
is screaming at my frozen watch.
Black Swifts have built their nests by now
behind waterfalls high in the Rockies.
The young swift is always hungry. The adults
soar out from the roaring water and course
the deep valleys. In extended storms
when insects are dormant the parents travel
a hundred miles or more to arc and flash
over warm prairie lakes. They return at night,
mouths bulging with butterflies,
to the nest and shrill screams.
A long meeting, several minutes nearer its end.

The Water Cycle

Deep-drenched along a trail in snow and showers,
you slow your pace and breathe decaying wood,
then merge into the drops that glaze the flowers,
the mist that slowly settles on your hood,

flow deep to find a way into the earthy
capillary rose from root to bloom,
turn color to ascend an arching pathway,
a rainbow beam made crystal off the moon,

float down inside the gliding flakes so narrow
the xylem and the phloem seem the same.
One dewdrop rosebush cloudbank shimmer rainbow,
one smoothness blend you melt into in rain.

A Mathematician Reflects

In these elliptical remarks I hope to translate
what I have achieved into familiar coordinates.
I wish I had been more linear,
rather than a set of vectors that,
when summed, place me near my origin.
Although I hoped for higher dimensions,
little is lost when I'm projected onto the plane.
If only I had formed a group,
but I lacked identity.
I wanted to be a strange attractor
living on the edge of chaos,
but my plot is classically simple.
Look for me in footnotes to other people's work.
I am approaching my limits asymptotically.
If I reach out, I can almost touch them.

Becoming Cat

It's not easy learning to hunt mice,
to stalk and leap, to hold one in my grasp,
to let it hope this kitty will be nice
as I smile and delicately clasp
it to my chest, then purr and dangle it,
let it stagger on uneasy legs,
and then with tender fondness strangle it
no matter how it cowers, squeals, or begs.

In all those deaths what is it I have learned
between my naps and dawn and evening meals?
What is it that my many kills have turned
from blood sport into wisdom? Time reveals
that what we do becomes us. It is that
that makes my daily mouse hunts into cat.

Dream Country

My waking and dream lives,
poised back to back,
scowl and invent excuses
to pace off ten steps,
turn and melt away.

Some things are found in both lives,
amphibious, like violets:
a flowery part and, in the dreams,
cubes reduced to the size of heartbeats.

When I tracked myself
into dream country
I followed hoofprints,
feathers, cuticles, sloughed-off skins
until, wrestling a familiar scarecrow,
I woke up deep inside his eyes.

Token Responses

In response to your pleas
for disaster relief,
here is a token.

In reply to your requests
for a useful education,
accept this token.

In acknowledgement of your need
for work at subsistence wages,
try collecting tokens.

Be the first on your block
to own the complete set of tokens—
a new one comes out every month.

You'll get a free album when you begin.
Your collection will only increase in value—
tokens will outlive silver and gold.

When you become an experienced collector
you will learn to prefer tokens
to less collectible types of responses.

Formalist Poet Contemplating an Orange

O accursed, unrhymable fruit!
Even the common apple has connections
to Snapple and a dappled trunk and root.
You'd work much better cut up into sections.

I hold you out before me. I can feel
your monochrome expanse of pitted skin.
I smell the fruity esters of your peel
and sense your form, the riddle wrapped within.

The Prince of Denmark studying a skull,
I ponder the enigma of the orange.
It has no rhyme and mocks me for a dull
and mortal hack aspiring to be more ang-
elic in the line-end breaks I pick.
Mid-word enjambment may have done the trick.

To A J

You thought to make your mark on life,
carefully incising your initials
on that smooth canvas.
Like you, the letters were young and green
and full of sap.
Some trees have no defense
against such violations.
This aspen was different.
Over the years, repelling
insects, diseases and winter frosts
you had opened it to,
the tree has obliterated your sign
with dark excrescence and bulging pustules,
a fate I see it also wished on you.

How It Used to Be

Whenever you came into view
a red spark leapt from me to you.
Our friends disliked it when we kissed—
no way for them to coexist.

You were theology and more,
were what they built the heavens for.
I was your eyes, you were my soul,
we each devoured the other whole.

And then the mighty river rolled.
You put on weight. I caught a cold.
We lay back on our aging bed.
"Not like it used to be," you said.

Caffe Di Siena

Monday

We choose our pastries from the display
of tiramisu, Napoleons, peanut butter brownies.
We take two coffees, white with sugar.
Shall we sit next to the opened laptop
or sit beside the quarreling couple?
We compromise on a table
near two hands holding the Newburyport News.
Her work is going well. Mine is exciting.
We'll stay in touch.
She asks whether we bus these dishes.
The air outside is breezy and cool.

Wednesday

I order a biscotti and he has coffee.
He says his new diet seems to be working.
We sit on display at the window.
He mugs at the pedestrians walking by.
He says it's been a difficult recession;
his business is limping and so is his marriage.
His heartbeat has some irregularities
and there's still that IRS thing.
He has a new venture—an Internet site—
linking Chinese programmers with mainland projects.
Would I like to get in at the start?
I sip the last of my coffee.
He asks whether we bus these dishes.
The air outside is heavy, threatening rain.

Saturday

I pick you up at the airport,
returning from your retreat in Orvieto.
You smell like Italy and the inside of an airplane.
We come here on the way home—
a taste of Italy in Newburyport.
Their cafes were nothing like this
(no Key Lime pie or two-tone brownies).
You show me photographs of wine cellars
and the monastery where you stayed.
There was good food and bad,
but look at these views of the valley!
We leave our half-eaten pastries on the table.
The air outside is bright from the rain.

The Exit Row

If you are seated in the exit row
you must be able to open the door
if we have crashed and your arm is broken
or a buckled fuselage is crushing your legs.
If you cannot understand these instructions
or do not wish to comply please request
another seat. The exit row
is not for the faint-hearted.
The perfect exit row passenger
has no imagination, a rugged physique,
and the unswerving will to turn a small wheel
carefully clockwise in the midst of smoke
and distracting screams.

Crossing Streams on Rocks

Each step counts,
even or odd depending on
which foot you are using and
which way you are headed when.
You can't plan before you begin.
You stay dry if you make
the one right move
each time you start to fall in.

The Juggler

I juggle what life gives me in an arc
that rises overhead: news from the media,
a subprime mortgage, marriage, a bad spark
plug, a three feet long encyclopedia.
I bite the apple as it flashes by,
lick the stamp and stick it to the letter,
poke thread into the silver needle's eye,
tune the engine so it idles better.
Then I myself am tossed up to the skies
to join the objects that I have just thrown.
I struggle to control them as I rise,
to make their orbits orbit me alone,
for I am juggled as I juggled them
and, juggled, must start juggling again.

Eight Translations of a Text by Washoe

Note: Washoe the chimpanzee was trained from birth to use human sign language. What follows are eight translations of one of Washoe's texts. Each is written by a different member of our on-line translation group.

The text, recorded by scientists one morning in her room after Washoe awoke, is a sequence of three signs that can be simplistically represented as "dark, light, food." All but one translator provided a brief comment on his or her approach to translating this text.

1 In the beginning there was darkness.
   Light spread over the face of the world
   and God created food.

   "Washoe was obviously signing a variation of the Creation story and I heightened that aspect of the text."

2 Darkness and light.
   My shadow crawls across the wall.
   A ripe banana!

   "The original is wonderfully terse. This was the first time I have expanded rather than compressing a text when converting it into haiku form."

3 Dark [not-light, depression, shade, shadow]
   then light [lamp, sun, bulb, not-dark]
   and food [banana, cereal, beetles, fruit, berries, grass, milk]

My note: As generally happens, NAT LANG TRANS submitted a translation but did not comment.

4 I dreamt I ate some fattened lice
 under the African sun.
 They tasted each of Paradise.
 I crunched them one by one.

 "I have a phobia of closed rooms and wanted to open up
 the scene, so I changed the location and added some content.
 I like the result."

5 My mind weeps in darkness on a prison cot
 while the light blinds my eyes.
 I eat my jailer's leavings.

 "Washoe's cry for help—that of an imprisoned intellect, the
 victim of human supremacists who bring shame on us all—
 can hardly be understood without tears."

6 From the dark hole, a bowl of fruit.
 The banana is the best.
 Its blunt form points at me, all mute,
 demanding interest.

 "Chimpanzees are highly sexual animals, a fact that freed me
 to use images I would not dare to employ in my own work."

7 The sun came in on little monkey feet,
 chattering insults at the night.
 It licked its swollen rump
 and left me a bowl of red berries.

 "I tried to cast the text in Bonobo terms, and was delighted to
 stumble on a metaphor that would communicate to them as
 well as to us."

8   I saw the best minds of my generation
    destroyed in laboratory cosmetics tests,
    hipsters beating on their bars like bongos,
    squinting into flickering fluorescent lights,
    grooving on chemicals from Princeton and Juarez—
    food colorings, carcinogens, amphetamines....

The extremely long text and comment are truncated at this point to comply with space requirements.

Final note: I have received Washoe's reply to our efforts, and our translations of it will appear in my next newsletter.

A.I.

Perhaps he lived an artificial life.
He felt the circuits glow beneath his skin
and studied programs to arouse his wife:
what words to say and how to help begin
their simulated melding on a bed
that might be there or might be made of dreams.
Perhaps the fiery wiring in his head
was changing what it is to what it seems.
He couldn't tell; his fuzzy logic lacked
the certainty of silicon and steel.
No upgrade could reverse the basic fact
that this is what his brain told him was real:
existence lived by dull organic rules
built from carbon, using faulty tools.

Over the Rainbow

Although your mind will be stretched very thin,
part of it left in the greyness behind,
part of it forward, guessing your future,

Although your head will swell from pressure changes,
the air in your ears pushing to escape,
sinuses discharging into your throat,

Although you will have just three inches to move in
and they will be filled by the sleeper in 21E
while your trapped eyes stare out for a hundred miles,

Although your senses, deprived, will attend to anything
and, no matter how many times you reread it,
Sky Mall will still be a book with no plot,

Even so you will enter the metal tube
to fly heavier than air over slipping time zones,
your body uncertain, spread across space,

Because there could be color on the other side,
somewhere over the rainbow and down
there could be peanuts filling pots with gold.

Philosophical Positions

Their divorce from reality was pronounced
more than two thousand years ago,
and so they are not tied to this earth
and have no visitation rights.
They float in their own world, self-contained,
their components glowing and insubstantial.
They breathe slowly,
inhaling premises and exhaling conclusions.
They communicate with each other,
trading accusations of inconsistency,
false suppositions and ungroundedness.
None of them mentions the elephant
holding up their universe: the fact
that no matter how hard they stare
into the surrounding blackness of space,
our world is not visible from theirs.

Lost in Space

Danger, Will Robinson! Although a machine,
I'm one whose goal is keeping you from harm
and I'm good at it. I know what they mean
behind their cunning grunts of peace, their warm

ear-puffs of steam proclaiming brotherhood.
Don't turn your back or all of that will cease,
this episode will be about the good
guys captured and the terms for your release:

the contents of the mother ship inside
a shuttle sent to them before night falls.
But I'll be hidden in it and I'll ride
unnoticed by their scanners, tap the walls,

locate a hidden entrance to a stair
(what good are stairs in space?) and find a tank
aglow with nutrients. Their brains float there!
I'll flip the switch and you'll have me to thank.

Projection

Lemmings do not march in masses to their death.
  We do.
Pigs do not by nature foul their sties.
  We do.
Who sees malice when the wolf pack
  hamstrings an elk,
Cruelty when the owl
  flays a wounded rabbit?
We do, we do, we do.

Swallows

One swallow soars by the window and is gone.
I run hot water into a bowl.

Two swallows soar by the window and are gone.
I scrub a platter and turn to rinse it,
then dry it with a blue towel.

Three swallows soar by the window and are gone.
I set the platter in its place on the shelf,
dry the water on the counter,
fold the towel and hang it up.

Strange, a day without any swallows.

Palace Tour

The Grounds

Because our country was starting in the old days,
  we are no longer cold.

Here is the ring of the many trees,
  given our king by his walkers.

The statue on your right is of a man.
  There is another on your left.

Here are the fundaments of the palace.
  They were broken and are still repairing.

Here are the ducks that make our country safe.
  They have been eating three times in our history.

The Rooms

The Holy Father was falling down
  in this room during the late fifteenth century.

Here the king was cutting off
  his ears by a count.

Here were the Hodwars, famous because
  they went from this room to the farms.

In the queen's room there were always men working
  and the king was having them killed.

The prince was living in this barrel
       for many weeks with food and waters.

The king's scientist was changing medals in this room,
       until he was one time exploding.

The Museum

This portrait is of the king's mother,
       before she was losing her eyes.

These medals like clothing were for
       soldiers so they did not feel sad.

There were many colors here
       until the invasion of 1653.

These are pictures of a great artist
       until the king was having him killed.

This shaped rock is our national,
       where the eagle is eating the bird.

Dawn

The early morning flaring of the skies
roars overhead as dawn grows out of black.
Through the dilated pupils of my eyes
the colors strike my nerves and, farther back,
inside my grayish, convoluted brain,
the neurons fire, the sweet endorphins flow.
I wonder what advantages we gain
in being so affected by this show.
Science can't explain the way dawn feels.
It's not the goal of natural selection.
No other species sees these reds and kneels
and looks inside itself for like perfection.
To other animals it's simply light.
Dawn's a human word and human sight.

An Underfunded Poem

With adequate resources, this would have been
a marvel composed of heroic couplets
with an omniscient narrator. Instead you have me,
and for this one I'll remain anonymous.

There could have been classical allusions
and references to the latest school of aesthetics.
Instead, here is a leaf symbolizing the past,
and one blade of green pointing to the future.

I sold off the rhymes to fund this last verse.
The power to my systems is being cut off.
Let's end with one small frog, croaking
beneath a tattered black rag standing in for night.

Remedial Math

Mr. Davis
Today we will do eight times seven
released at the whiteboard
to flutter at drawn windows
until you let it in

Julie
How do you work the kind of example
where apples shimmer in summer heat
and nobody eats them because he's gone
and some man is kissing your mother
between you and the table?

Kurt
Do you plus or minus hens
after foxes have run off
choking on feathers and blood?

Sarah
The wren's song
sizzles like rain
on a potbellied stove
and all the pines
point away from themselves.
What good is math?

Mr. Davis
Chant them like mantras
as you jog, sleep, eat.
There is beatitude
in knowing your tables

Still Life with Gunfight

Around and through the oranges and figs
the silenced bullets fly.
Bananas turn to pulp, the missiles' whiz
the only sound as they go by.

The toppled apples dance a dance that's felt
rather than heard or seen.
A shattered bunch of grapes begins to melt
into an open magazine.

The hero tries to aim above the fruit.
The villain doesn't care.
For them, the unaware, the point is moot:
the juice that used to be a pear

does not know why one tangerine was missed,
nor does it know why it ceased to exist.

Two Paths to Bliss

His
A slice of bread, a glass of wine, and you
off to a meeting while I watch kung fu.

Hers
True love is love that ever stronger grows
if you're mall walking while I try on clothes.

This Is Not a Poem

These are not poetic lines and this is not a poem.
These are sentences set off so each one stands alone.
This is not a couplet and it isn't meant to rhyme.
It's not metered, can't be scanned, is not in two-beat time.
This is not a sonnet; what you're reading has no form.
It's prose as blank as Lear's was, raging in his thunderstorm.
This is not a paradox; there's nothing deep to see.
It mimics Escher and Magritte in their simplicity.

There's no external reason causing these lines to exist.
If you dissent then think again and grasp the point you've missed.
They flow from the depthless well of my integrity.
Obeying their own laws, they are and will and must be free.
They stand in formless protest of the tyranny of style.
They light the far horizons, help us ponder for a while.

These lines go where none have gone; watch them as they roam.
There is no name for what they do, and this is not a poem.

The Woman in the Cigarette Ads

Deported now, in her time
she was the model American woman.
She married Philip Morris but we knew
she always carried a torch for Winston.
Camel's hair coats and Virginia Slim—
She came to work dressed as a Player.
They lived in Marlboro but he commuted
to Chesterfield. They summered in Newport.
She was upbeat, Kool, and Lucky.
Strike up a dirge, for she is exiled
to the foggy land of Parliament.
On a Lark, she walks in clouds.
Footballers run Pall-Mall after her,
rapt in her nimbus, the subtle Merit
of her blowing hair's Old Gold.

Peano's Postulates

How does a finite brain
grasp the concept? Infinity
has been defined
as being able to add one
each time you are given a number,
as if a finite action, repeatable,
created something beyond it,
as if being able to love
any thing you are given
proved the existence
of infinite love.

Like Meeting Like

The deadliest of weaponry is lost
when met with its own special type of force.
Diamond scratches diamond. Two swords crossed
will dull each other's edges in due course.
What they are can bring them to an end
while what they aren't will fall before their might.
With steel on steel the steel will surely bend.
A bullet splits a bullet in mid-flight.
That's why I avoid fanning my passion
to the level yours is flaming at.
If we touched, the action and reaction
would leave us both burned out and lying flat.
It's better if you blaze while I just smolder.
We can reverse our roles as we grow older.

The Celebration

One car honked behind me,
then another on my right,
then all the cars were honking, sending up
a rolling wall of sound.
The drivers left their vehicles and danced
with pedestrians in the street.
Firecrackers echoed in an alleyway.
Shadowy rooftop figures shot rifles
for more than thirty minutes.
Next day I asked what had happened.
A celebration? my colleagues said.
We are a passionate people.
Perhaps you were caught in a traffic jam.

The Perfect Metaphor

How to write the most effective,
clear, specific, telling image,
a single detail that captures
all of life, its meaning, more?

I go outside where things are larger:
streets and trees and far beyond them
unseen worlds live long and prosper
amid galaxies, gas clouds and suns.

Sparrows avoid me on the sidewalk,
intently searching for their crumbs.

Winter Solstice

The daisy days
    have dropped in petals
        one by one

and now the yellow
    face above
        has no more rays to give.

It loves us not,
    it loves us yes,
        the sun.

City Voices

Cab Driver
For your convenience
I'll take the scenic route,
won't even ask.

Foreman
If you don't watch them
they'll take advantage.
I know I did.

Street Sweeper
If I ever go crazy
I'll shoot random passersby
who are chewing gum.

Nurse
Twelve times today
my children called
for help with math.

Pretzel Vendor
I've been here longer
than every store on the block
but they want me to move.

Mayor
If I ever go crazy
I'll strangle a council member
in mid-objection.

Window Arranger
Remember that
you view my work
through your reflection.